CW00474262

THE ANAYA **SUN SIGN** *COMPANIONS*

LIBRA

24 September-23 October

CELESTINE O'RYAN

ANAYA PUBLISHERS LIMITED
LONDON

First published in Great Britain in 1991 by
Anaya Publishers Ltd., Strode House, 44-50 Osnaburgh Street, London NW1 3ND

Copyright © Anaya Publishers Ltd 1991

ASTROLOGICAL CONSULTANT Jan Kurrels

Managing Editor	Judy Martin
Art Director	Nigel Osborne
Designers	Sally Stockwell
	Anne Clue
Illustrators	Marion Appleton
	David Ashby
	Lorraine Harrison
	Tony Masero
Indexer	Peter Barber

British Library Cataloguing in Publication Data
O'Ryan, Celestine
   Libra. – (Anaya sun sign companions).
   1. Astrology
   I. Title
   133.52
   ISBN 1-85470-096-0

TYPESET IN GREAT BRITAIN BY MIDFORD TYPESETTING LTD, LONDON
COLOUR ORIGINATION IN SINGAPORE BY COLUMBIA OFFSET LTD
PRINTED IN SINGAPORE BY TIMES OFFSET LTD

CONTENTS

LIBRA

*Most people know their own sun sign, and you know
that yours is Libra, but do you appreciate its full
impact on every area of your life? Your* Sun Sign
Companion *is a guide to the many pleasures and
preferences that are specific to you as a Libran subject.
Your personality profile is here – and much more.
You can find out not only where you fit into the grand
astrological scheme and the ways the other zodiac signs
connect with your own, but also discover the delights of
the Libran foods that are your special delicacies; the
plants that you should grow in your garden to enhance
your Libran moods; the animals that you appreciate
for their affinities to your sign and the pets that you as
a Libran can easily love and live with; the ways in
which you need to take care of your body, and how
your health and well-being may be affected by the fact
that you were born under Libra.*

The fascinating range of this Sun Sign Companion *explains your temperament, your actions and the ways you live your life in zodiacal terms. You have a sociable and diplomatic nature and your special element – Libran air – makes you clear-headed and far-sighted; your planetary ruler Venus, queen of love, encourages creative alliances. You have singular connections with the powers of the Earth itself – its gemstones, metals and crystals. And your zodiacal profile is underlined by your Libran connections to the ancient arts of the Runes and the Tarot. This book provides you with the intriguing mosaic of influences, interests and attributes that build into the total picture of yourself as a Libran. More than any other zodiacal guide, your* Sun Sign Companion *reveals to you the inherent fun and enjoyment of life under Libra.*

THE ZODIAC

hen the ancient astrologers studied the sky at night, they tracked the obvious motion and changing shape of the Moon, but noted two other phenomena: the frosty grandeur of the fixed stars and the different movements of the five observable planets. Mercury, Venus, Mars, Jupiter and Saturn moved and weaved about the night sky in repeating patterns, always within the same narrow strip of the heavens. And in the day time, the Sun could be seen progressing along the centre of this strip on its apparent orbit. Most of the action, celestially speaking, appeared to take place in a restricted

heavenly corridor. Astronomers and astrologers therefore gave priority to this ribbon of sky, and noted what else appeared in it.

Sharing the strip were twelve fixed star constellations, known from ancient times. They were Aries the Ram, Taurus the Bull, Gemini the Twins, Cancer the Crab, Leo the Lion, Virgo the Virgin, Libra the Balance, Scorpius the Scorpion, Sagittarius the Archer, Capricornus the Goat, Aquarius the Water Carrier and Pisces the Fishes. As most of the constellations are named after sentient creatures, the Greeks called this band of sky the zodiac, from their word meaning images of animals or living beings.

In astronomical terms, the constellations take up varying amounts of sky and exhibit different degrees of brightness. Astrologically, they are assigned equal prominence and importance, and are given equal 30-degree arcs of the celestial band. These are the signs of the zodiac, and the starting point on the celestial circle is 0 degrees Aries, which was the point of the vernal equinox over 4000 years ago when the zodiac was established.

The celestial jostling along the zodiacal corridor is explained by the fact that the planets orbit the Sun roughly in the same plane. Imagine yourself at the centre of a race track, timing a group of runners as they lap the circuit, each one running at a different pace and in a different lane. Soon you would be able to predict when each one would pass you, especially if you noted down landmarks along the spectator stands behind the runners.

In the same way, astrologers pinpoint the position and motion of any planet, using the zodiac band as a reference grid. Interpretation of the effects of planetary power filtered through the zodiac grid is the enduring fascination of astrology. The planets are extremely powerful, as represented by their having been awarded the names and attributes of the gods.

ZODIACAL INFLUENCES

 our sun sign is the zodiac sign that the Sun, the most powerful of the heavenly bodies, appears to be passing through from our viewpoint on Earth at the time of your birth. It takes the Sun one year to progress through all the signs, and it is the Sun's huge power, filtered through each sign in turn, that etches the broad character templates of each sign. Over the centuries, each sign has acquired its own repertory of characteristics and personality traits, a seamless blend of archetypal myth and particular observation. So now we can talk about, say, a 'typical Libra' with the expectation that others will know what we mean. However, fine tuning and modification of the individual personality are dictated by two conditions at the time of birth – the positions of the Moon and planets in the zodiac and the nature of the ascendant, the sign rising on the eastern horizon at the moment of birth.

The Earth spins counter-clockwise daily on its axis, but to us it appears that the Sun, stars and planets wheel overhead from east to west. Within this framework, the zodiac passing overhead carries with it one sign every two hours; therefore the degree of the ascendant changes likewise, which explains why two people born on the same day can have such varying personalities. The influence of the ascending sign, and any planet positioned in it, has a strong bearing on the formation of the personality. A Libran with Pisces in the ascendant is quite a different kettle of fish to one with Capricorn ascending.

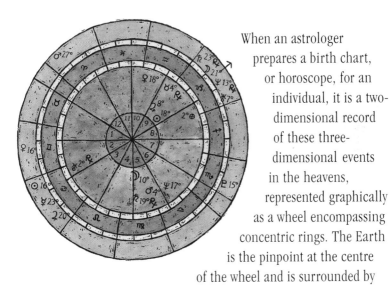

When an astrologer prepares a birth chart, or horoscope, for an individual, it is a two-dimensional record of these three-dimensional events in the heavens, represented graphically as a wheel encompassing concentric rings. The Earth is the pinpoint at the centre of the wheel and is surrounded by twelve fixed segments representing the zodiacal Houses, the areas of life in which planetary influences will manifest themselves. The outer circle of the chart represents the moving zodiacal corridor, divided into its twelve segments – the signs of the zodiac.

The predictability of the planets' movements has enabled astrologers to create tables, known as Ephemerides, of the planetary positions past, present and future. Once the positions of the Sun, Moon and planets have been established for a specific time, and a particular subject, the astrologer can assess and interpret what effects the planets will have, how they will enhance, diminish or frustrate each other's powers, and which areas of the subject's life will come under their particular influences. And all of this information is blended with the astrologer's understanding of the sun sign personality, the broad framework of individuality in zodiacal terms.

THE LIBRA PERSONALITY

ibra is the seventh sign of the zodiac. Sociable, good natured, optimistic, diplomatic and cheerful, Libra is a born charmer, making use of naturally winning ways to defuse quarrels and smooth over life's rough spots. Lovers of the good things in life, refined and graceful, Librans have built-in poise. In fact, poise is what Librans are all about – bringing order out of chaos, whether it is reconciling intransigent opponents or reviving a cold, unlovely house by dressing it in warm, welcoming decor.

Venus, the planet of love and harmony, rules Libra, and implacable Saturn, known to ancient astrologers as the Great Leveller, is exalted, or extra-powerful in Libra. It is Libra's mission in life to reconcile these planetary powers, tempering the cold steel of justice with the gentle rain of compassion, blending beauty, truth and justice into a harmonious whole.

A keen sense of fair play makes Libra a militant champion of the underdog, but Librans do not go in for altruistic martyrdom: give and take is the Libran principle. Librans give freely, extravagantly even, of themselves, but keep mental tabs on the ledger and expect to be repaid in kind; sadly they are often disappointed by others' inability to match their generosity.

Libra cannot live with loneliness, and needs the company of friends, the intimacy of lovers, the secure partnership of marriage. Fortunately, attracting friends and lovers is no problem for handsome, generous, fun-loving, life-enhancing Libra.

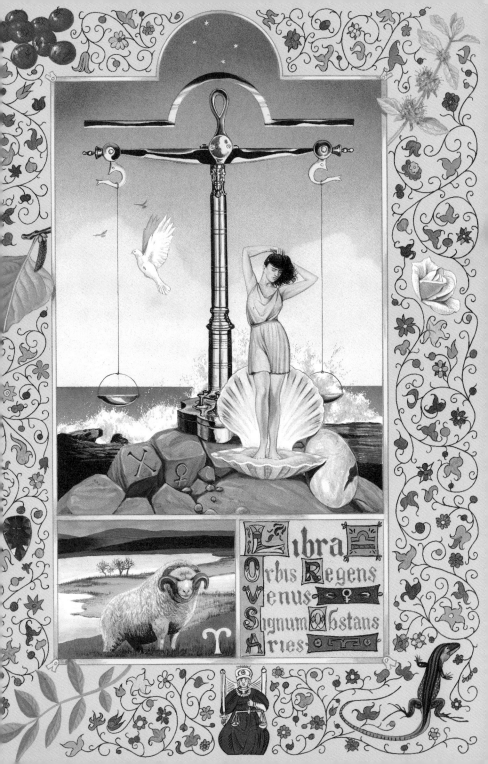

Libra
Orbis Regens
Venus ♀
Signum Obstans
Aries

THE PLANETARY RULER

ncient astrologers named the five planets they could see in the night sky after the five most powerful classical gods; naturally, the planets took on the attributes and associations of the gods, and a pleasingly symmetrical system was devised to distribute this planetary power throughout the zodiac.

The Sun and Moon, being the most dazzling lights, ruled one sun sign each (Leo and Cancer). The remaining ten signs managed under the shared patronage of the five planets. Mercury presided over Gemini and Virgo, Venus over Taurus and Libra, Mars over Aries and Scorpio, Jupiter over Sagittarius and Pisces, and Saturn over Aquarius and Capricorn.

When more planets were discovered after the invention of the telescope in 1610, a reshuffle became necessary. Uranus

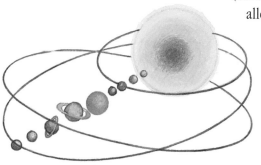

(discovered in 1781) was allocated to Aquarius, Neptune (1836) was thought appropriate for Pisces, and Pluto (1930) now broods over Scorpio. This has unbalanced the symmetry: the search is on for other planets to share the burden with Venus and Mercury. Indeed, the asteroid Chiron, discovered in 1977 looping the void between Saturn and Uranus, is considered by some astrologers to be the suitable governor of Virgo.

The planetary power behind Libra comes from Venus, queen of harmony. Venus represents desire, love, affection, harmony,

 partnership, fruitfulness, creativity, beauty, peace and plenty. It promotes harmony and understanding, cooperation and sharing, a love of beauty and the desire and ability to create beautiful things and fruitful alliances. Adversely, it can encourage impractical dreaming, weak-willed over-indulgence, foolish romanticism and too much dependence on the goodwill of others.

Astronomically, Venus is the second planet from the Sun in the solar system, our nearest planetary neighbour. More or less the same size as Earth, and for centuries considered to be our sister planet, it takes only 225 days to orbit the Sun. Swathed in dense, reflective cloud, Venus is the brightest object in the heavens after the Sun and Moon. It is easily visible to the naked eye; in the dawn skies, it sparkles as the Morning Star; and from dusk it glimmers as the Evening Star, long after the Sun has set.

In classical mythology, Venus is a complex deity, the multi-faceted and mysterious female principle, representing at once sexual desire, love, harmony, fertility and creativity. Venus is the all-embracing Roman name for the Greek goddesses Aphrodite (love and desire) and Demeter (fertility). Venus had many lovers but her enduring passion was for Ares, or Mars, the god of War.

PATTERNS IN THE STARS

 tar pictures, or images of the constellations, are formed in the eye of the beholder. What we see as a neighbourly cluster is usually an optical illusion, the stars in the group being many light years apart. Even so, the urge to impose a friendly pattern on the frosty immensity of the night sky, to link the stars with the myths and legends on Earth, has been irresistible to all cultures. Different cultures make out different pictures, and the results are sometimes inscrutable – searching for Leo, say, you will look in vain for the shape of a lion pricked out in stars against the dark backcloth of the night sky.

The zodiac constellations were among the first to be made out, as they were the main star groups that formed the background to the moving planets, providing a useful reference grid to plot planetary movements. These gave their names to the signs of the

zodiac, although they spread unevenly across the sky and are not tidily confined to the equal 30-degree segments of the imaginary zodiac band. Most stars are known by their Arabic names, and the star that shone brightest in each constellation when Arabic astrologers first compiled their star catalogues was designated its alpha.

The constellation that gave its name to the seventh sign of the zodiac is the southern star group Libra the Scales, or Balance, an undistinguished constellation which fits neatly into the width of the zodiacal band, the belt of sky that threads through each of the zodiacal constellations forming the pathway of the planets. Libra has four dim stars and one of those, Zubenalgubi, Sigma Libra, was once assigned to Scorpius as Gamma Scorpionis. In fact, the whole of Libra was originally assigned to its magnificent neighbour, Scorpius the Scorpion. The ancient Arabs and Greeks called it Chelae Scorpionis, the claws of the Scorpion. It later joined the exclusive zodiac club as a constellation in its own right.

If the constellation is obscure, the myth behind it is even less clear. Libra is the starry image of a balance or set of scales. The Babylonian name for the constellation was *Zibanitu*, which originally meant horn or claws, but later came to mean scales, as this was the time of the year when the harvested grain was weighed. It was the Babylonians who first detached the claws from the scorpion and recognized Libra as a constellation in its own right. The idea was consolidated by the Egyptians, who weighed their harvest and levied their taxes when the Moon was full in Libra; there are also associations with the ceremonial weighing of dead souls by the Egyptian gods Anubis, Osiris and Thoth.

THE ATTRACTION OF OPPOSITES

n astrological terms, polarity describes the strong complementary relationship between signs that are exactly opposite each other on the zodiac circle, 180 degrees or six signs apart. These signs share the same gender – masculine or feminine – and the same quality – cardinal, fixed or mutable – and so share the ways they look at the world and shape their energy. Characteristics and interests complement each other or harmonize on different scales.

Relationships between polar signs are often very satisfying and fruitful, especially in the context of work. A clue to this affinity lies with the elements governed by each sign. The mathematics of polarity mean that earth signs oppose only water signs, and that fire opposes only air. Fire and air signs therefore encourage and inspire each other – fire cannot burn without air and air needs heat to rise. Earth and water signs conspire together creatively – earth without water is unfruitful, water unconfined by earth wastes

its energy in diffusion – and together they make mud, rich material for any creative process.

Six signs away from well-mannered, well-balanced, harmonious Libra, the diplomat of the zodiac, we find headstrong Aries, the leader of the pack who makes decisions at the snap of a finger. Impetuous, reckless Aries, who puts his head down and charges joyously full tilt at life's hurdles can be terrifying to scrupulous Libra, who weighs up the pros and cons, takes all viewpoints into consideration, and would far rather sit on a fence than leap over it.

Below the surface, however, a shared and complementary shaping energy is at work, the cardinal energy of creation. Both Libra and Aries preside over momentous times of the year, the autumn and spring equinoxes, when the Sun makes its decisive move from one hemisphere to the other, a time of new beginnings. Libra, the air sign, fans out its creative energy to reach as many people as possible. Aries, the fire sign, burns with a hard, gemlike flame, intent on getting the individual show on the road. Libra's gentle but determined energy diffraction prevents the intense Arian energy from burning so fiercely that it destroys itself and all around it.

The complementary aspect of polarity is also seen in the characteristics traditionally associated with the two signs. Both are keen to promote action to an end, Libra by bringing people together, promoting harmony and collective action, Aries by rushing out and doing it in person. Libra integrates the individual's contribution into the wider context of society, Aries energizes the individual so that he or she will have something to contribute.

THE SYMBOLS OF THE ZODIAC

 ver since astrology began, there has been a kind of astrological shorthand, a set of symbols or ideograms called glyphs. Glyphs make the language of astrology universal and available to people who have no literary tradition. They also make it a lot easier to draw up a birth chart, being a convenient form of notation, especially when planets are clustered in one area of the chart.

Each of the zodiac signs has its own glyph, as do the planets. They have evolved over centuries, and so are now freighted with symbolism, not simply convenient codes.

Today, the glyph for Libra is a pleasingly harmonious graphic pattern, two parallel horizontal lines, the top line interrupted in the middle by a small semicircle. The graphic thread linking the various glyphs that have represented Libra through the ages is remarkably consistent. Early Egyptians

went in for a hieroglyph shaped like the cross-section of a ball in a cup, probably a representation of the soul of a dead person being weighed in the scale-pan presided over by the gods of the underworld, Anubis and Thoth. The Greeks had two symbols, one a pared-down line drawing of the Egyptian hieroglyph, the other an even more simplified version, like the letter E laid horizontally. Medieval astrologers also used two versions, one a rather ill-defined squiggle of two parallel but curving lines, the other a prototype of the modern glyph, but without the bottom line.

There is a special fascination in studying the glyphs to see what other symbolism may be contained within them. The Libra glyph is a very clear, strong graphic image of a clear, strong concept: equilibrium. It is a simple, symmetrical representation of the disturbance and restoration of balance – harmony interrupted and regained.

The planets also have their glyphs, and the Venus symbol is familiar to all biology students. It is the symbol of the feminine principle, a circle mounted on a cross.

THE HOUSE OF LIBRA

he twelve Houses are an intellectual concept, not a physical reality, an expression of all the aspects of human life and experience, from the self to the infinite. Each is associated with a sign of the zodiac, sharing its planetary ruler and elemental energy. However, the Houses are fixed and constant – they are represented by the central

numbered segments on a birth chart – and the signs and planets pass through them. They are the channels through which planetary and zodiacal energies flow and indicate which area of life is the focus of particular zodiacal influence at any one time.

Libra, being the seventh sign of the zodiac, is associated with the Seventh House, which is also overseen by Libra's planetary ruler Venus. Like Libra, the Seventh House is permeated with air energy, and therefore concerns itself with mental and intellectual activity, all levels of communication and social interaction. In particular, it is concerned with close relationships – work colleagues, business partnerships, love affairs and marriage. The Seventh House is an intimate, congenial place, somewhere agreeable to entertain close friends and lovers.

When Venus is in the Seventh House on a Libra birth chart, it
magnifies the instinctive Libra talent for personal relationships,
bringing the powerful, positive emotions and desire for harmony
that promote successful business mergers and fruitful marriages.

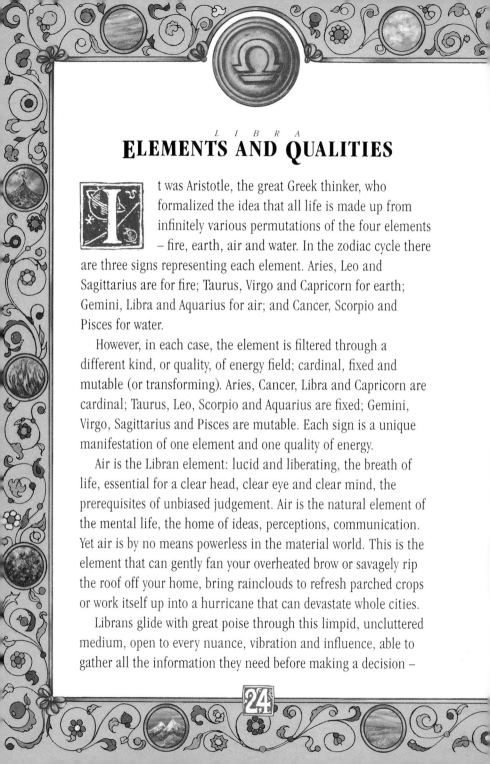

ELEMENTS AND QUALITIES

t was Aristotle, the great Greek thinker, who formalized the idea that all life is made up from infinitely various permutations of the four elements – fire, earth, air and water. In the zodiac cycle there are three signs representing each element. Aries, Leo and Sagittarius are for fire; Taurus, Virgo and Capricorn for earth; Gemini, Libra and Aquarius for air; and Cancer, Scorpio and Pisces for water.

However, in each case, the element is filtered through a different kind, or quality, of energy field; cardinal, fixed and mutable (or transforming). Aries, Cancer, Libra and Capricorn are cardinal; Taurus, Leo, Scorpio and Aquarius are fixed; Gemini, Virgo, Sagittarius and Pisces are mutable. Each sign is a unique manifestation of one element and one quality of energy.

Air is the Libran element: lucid and liberating, the breath of life, essential for a clear head, clear eye and clear mind, the prerequisites of unbiased judgement. Air is the natural element of the mental life, the home of ideas, perceptions, communication. Yet air is by no means powerless in the material world. This is the element that can gently fan your overheated brow or savagely rip the roof off your home, bring rainclouds to refresh parched crops or work itself up into a hurricane that can devastate whole cities.

Librans glide with great poise through this limpid, uncluttered medium, open to every nuance, vibration and influence, able to gather all the information they need before making a decision –

or, in many cases, putting off a decision. They also love the idea that they can reach out unimpeded to everybody and include them all in their harmonious vision of the world.

Libran energy is cardinal. Cardinal people are natural leaders because they are an ever-renewable source of their own energy, whatever kind it is. Venus, Libra's ruler, is the daughter of the great sky god Uranus, born from the foam of the ocean when Uranus was unmanned by Saturn and his blood dripped into the sea. Libra therefore has a direct connection to an endless supply of the pure, unpolluted air of sweet reason, the transparent medium which allows beauty and harmony to shine through it.

THE ZODIAC GARDEN

A Libran riding in the unostentatious luxury of a modestly sized but well-appointed automobile, to the discreet accompaniment of baroque music on the sound system, will want to look out upon civilized countryside – a long, straight poplar-lined French road, perhaps, with a château shimmering in the distance. Better still, romantic Librans love to be rowed or punted down a peaceful river

by a besotted admirer. But the favourite outdoor environment for Librans is the cunningly improved grounds of a stately home, an exercise in artless elegance and elegant artfulness. Librans can well appreciate the vision of the great landscape gardeners of the past, who brought sweet order and symmetry out of wild uncaring nature, and bequeathed the best of their efforts to generations yet to come.

Libra's own garden will not be so grand, but will have a certain formality, enlivened by a dash of the unusual. Hidden behind stately irises, delphinium beds and hydrangea bushes – Libra favours blue flowers – there may be a lawn of pennyroyal, flooding the air with minty fragrance when walked on. Libra likes the balance of indoors and outdoors; whereas the Libran home will be full of plants, the Libran garden is often civilized by furniture and features: pergolas, fountains, love seats, classical statuary, gazebos, a dovecote – perhaps a bower of white roses to dally in, since the white rose belongs to Libra's planetary ruler, Venus. As Libra's idea of gardening is to drift languidly through the green shade picking sweet-smelling flowers – campanulas, sweet peas, hyacinths – perhaps a gardener who could take care of the spadework would be a good investment. Then Libra can recline on the padded garden swing with a close friend, sipping mint julep and looking beautiful.

Impartial Libra treats the garden like a living room, and the living room like a garden. Inside the Libran home there will be an abundance of foliage, bulbs in various stages of development, pretty herbs, even a strawberry tower. And there will always be fresh flowers, beautifully arranged: pale roses if Libra is in the money (or has an ardent Taurean admirer); bluebells, forget-me-nots and poppies if the bank is temporarily broken. For Libra follows the ancient Chinese proverb: 'If you have two loaves, sell one and buy a flower.' Libra cannot live by bread alone.

ASTROLOGY AND THE ARK

he word zodiac comes from the Greek word for animal or living creature, and many of the signs are symbolized by animals. Libra, however, is represented by the abstract concept of the balance. Sometimes this is interpreted as the image of a clear-eyed young woman holding a set of scales, ready to assess and make judgement on the frailties and preoccupations of the human race rather than interest herself in the instinctive processes of the animal kingdom.

Yet Libra is traditionally associated with lizards and small reptiles. There is something very Libran about slow-blinking lizards, lazing motionless on their hot rocks, apparently meditating on some highly ancient wisdom, taking a lifetime to decide whether to move, and scuttling like sudden lightning when they do. Some are extremely beautiful, their bright, enamelled colours turning them into living jewellery that is very satisfying to Libra's aesthetic sense. Cleopatra, who threw away her empire for love, must surely have been much influenced by Libra; when she wanted to end her life, she chose to do so with an asp. And the

chameleon could be described as the most Libran creature on this planet, a lizard who can blend in with any background, harmony taken to its logical conclusion.

With their highly developed aesthetic sense, Librans appreciate the beauty of animals in the wild – the fearful symmetry of Blake's bright-burning tiger, for instance – but prefer to study it on film or television rather than suffer the discomforts of the trail. They may also find an affinity with solemn, round-eyed owls, the bird sacred to Athene, the Greek goddess of wisdom and justice. And some Librans are fascinated by the slow-motion balancing act of the sloth.

On the whole, Librans prefer the company of other people to that of animals, and realize that dependent, demanding pets may disturb the even balance of their lives and restrict their freedom. However, an independent, self-possessed, luxury-loving cat may find an agreeable home with Libra, perhaps a beautiful, well-behaved, long-legged Burmese.

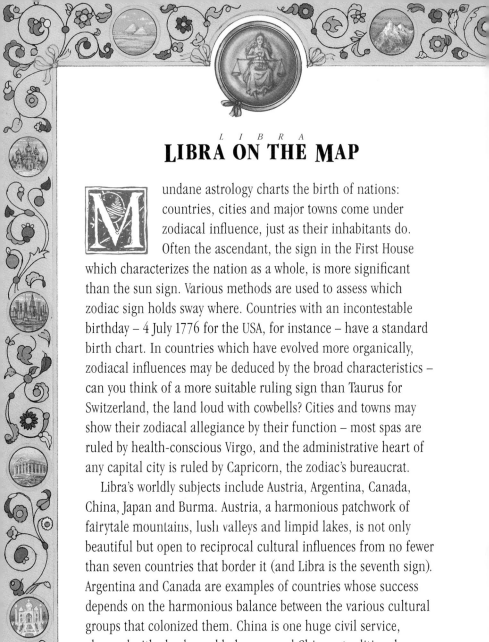

LIBRA ON THE MAP

Mundane astrology charts the birth of nations: countries, cities and major towns come under zodiacal influence, just as their inhabitants do. Often the ascendant, the sign in the First House which characterizes the nation as a whole, is more significant than the sun sign. Various methods are used to assess which zodiac sign holds sway where. Countries with an incontestable birthday – 4 July 1776 for the USA, for instance – have a standard birth chart. In countries which have evolved more organically, zodiacal influences may be deduced by the broad characteristics – can you think of a more suitable ruling sign than Taurus for Switzerland, the land loud with cowbells? Cities and towns may show their zodiacal allegiance by their function – most spas are ruled by health-conscious Virgo, and the administrative heart of any capital city is ruled by Capricorn, the zodiac's bureaucrat.

Libra's worldly subjects include Austria, Argentina, Canada, China, Japan and Burma. Austria, a harmonious patchwork of fairytale mountains, lush valleys and limpid lakes, is not only beautiful but open to reciprocal cultural influences from no fewer than seven countries that border it (and Libra is the seventh sign). Argentina and Canada are examples of countries whose success depends on the harmonious balance between the various cultural groups that colonized them. China is one huge civil service, obsessed with checks and balances; and Chinese traditional

medicine is based on the concept of keeping the body at equilibrium and in harmony with nature. And Japan's culture is shaped by restrained, balanced beauty, a culture that transforms tea-time into an elegant, elaborate ceremony. Libra also rules a region. Alsace-Lorraine in France, a symmetrical balance of French and German culture and cuisine; it is even shaped like a number seven on the map.

Cities under Libra include Vienna, where music and delicious cakes meet socially; Antwerp, the jewel-box of Europe and the home of Rubens, the painter *par excellence* of voluptuous female flesh; Copenhagen, salty old Queen of the Sea; Nottingham, famous for its beautiful lace and home to Robin Hood, the outlaw champion who aimed to redress the social balance and redistribute wealth. Other Libran cities are Leeds, Lisbon, Frankfurt and Freiburg.

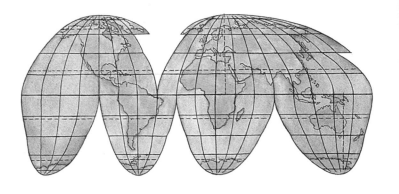

EARTH'S BOUNTY

ood plants associated with Libra include tomatoes, beans, asparagus, strawberries, quinces and all kinds of pears, foods that appeal to both the Libran aptitude for light luxurious nourishment and the Libran eye for beauty. Beans are a nutritionist's dream, delivering protein and energy with minimal fat: and the climbing red flowers of runner beans are almost good enough to eat. Asparagus (which 'stirreth up lust') and strawberries deliciously combine the erotic with the exotic and are wonderful eaten together, preferably as a picnic on a reed-screened punt with Libra's current love.

Buttery, succulent pears make a dessert fit for any love feast.

Tomatoes and quinces bring Libra's ruler Venus irresistibly to mind: when tomatoes arrived in Europe via Italy in the sixteenth century, they were called 'love apples' or 'golden apples' and credited with sensational aphrodisiac powers; another candidate for the Golden Apple award is the quince, an ancient fruit cultivated since Roman times. The Golden Apples of classical myth grew on Hera's tree, guarded by the Hesperides;

Hercules heroically stole three for his Eleventh Labour, but then dedicated them to Athene, the goddess of wisdom, who in turn returned them to their tree and restored harmony on Olympus.

Eating with Libra is a treat: you will be cosseted and indulged in the soft glow of candlelight; there will be flowers, light classical music, congenial company and an attentive host. The food will be light and delicious, featuring lots of fruit and balancing contrasting tastes in the same dish – sweet and sour, perhaps, or a Moroccan fruit and meat *tajine*. Heavy cream sauces, rich puddings and masses of starch will not feature, but Libra will not be able to resist a box (or more) of tempting handmade chocolates.

Of course, Libra loves dining out, whether it is with the paramour of the moment or a group of good friends, in a restaurant or at another's home. It's the company and ambience that matter most to Libra: the cuisine is secondary (although it must be good). Libra goes for welcoming, relaxing places to eat, neither too haughty, too stylish nor too spartan; unusual places catch the Libran imagination – lunching on a luxury yacht for example – and Librans adore picnics.

A HEAVENLY HERBAL

erbs and the heavens have been linked forever; for many centuries, herbs were the only medicine, and the gathering and application of them were guided by the planets. Doctors would learn the rudiments of astrology as a matter of course – Hippocrates claimed that 'a physician without a knowledge of astrology had no right to call himself a physician'.

Healing plants and their ruling planets were often linked via the elements – fire, water, air and earth. Mars, for example, a hot fiery planet, self-evidently rules over hot, fiery plants such as mustard. Herbs that cure the ills of particular parts of the body are ruled by the planet that governs that part of the body. Plants are also assigned according to what they look like. For example, walnuts, which look like tiny models of the brain, are ruled by Mercury, the planet which rules the brain.

All herbs are more effective if they are gathered on a day ruled by their patron planet, especially at dawn, when they are fat with sap drawn up by the beams of the Moon, or at dusk, after a day basking in the strengthening rays of the Sun.

The Libran herbs are mint and cayenne, the hot spicy pepper made from dried ground red chillies. Both are famous for arousing and stimulating appetites of all kinds. Cayenne pepper is used to spike powerful cough medicines. (Venus's subjects suffer from throat problems occasionally.) Mint is a wonderfully even-handed Libran herb: it makes mouthwatering sauces to enliven your main course – and provides a soothing digestive afterwards, even a cure for toothache if indulgence has got out of hand. Medieval herbalists considered that the very scent of mint aroused joyful lust. After-dinner mints combine the digestive and seductive properties in one delicious treat. There are many mint varieties – spearmint, watermint, peppermint, applemint, pennyroyal and catmint, which drives cats into an ecstatic frenzy. Mint is named for Mentha, the adulterous nymph, caught *in flagrante delicto* with Pluto, god of the underworld, by his wife, Persephone, who lost no time in turning Mentha into the pungent herb while she was still glowing with the fires of love: a suitable fable for zodiac subjects ruled by Venus, shared by Libra and Taurus.

THE CELESTIAL BODY

ach part of the body comes under the influence of a different zodiac sign. Libra, appropriately, rules the kidneys, the body's balancing act. Like Libra, the kidneys work very hard without any apparent effort, processing and recycling almost 200 litres of blood a day, filtering out the bad and retaining the good, eliminating poisons and reabsorbing essential nutrients. They also help to keep the balance of mineral salts in the blood exactly right; if this balance is upset, one of the symptoms may be an inexplicable headache. This should not surprise Librans, as the head is ruled by Libra's polar sign, Aries. Hotheaded Aries also rules the adrenal glands, which perch on top of the kidneys and pump out adrenalin.

The planets are thought to govern body systems, and Libra's ruler, Venus, is associated with the kidneys, lower back, throat and the parathyroid glands, four little glands just behind the thyroid which regulate the balance of phosphorous and calcium.

The sensitive balance of Libran health is easily upset, and Librans should beware of overindulgence: the good things in life are almost irresistible to pleasure-oriented Venus subjects. Libra loves to look good, and Libra is a good-looking sign, but is unwilling to suffer in order to be beautiful. A self-pampering session in an elegant health spa is the preferred Libran option, or dancing perhaps (with a partner, of course), or a Sunday morning run with friends, ending up in the café or bar. After a hard day charming the world, Librans should treat themselves to a slow, sensuous massage with a gorgeous oil such as sandalwood, ylang ylang or patchouli.

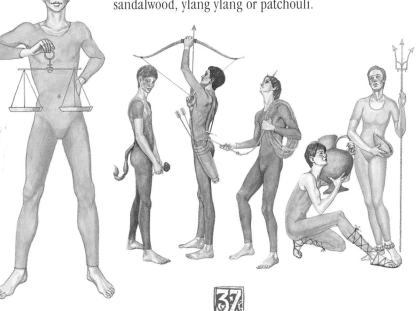

35

THE STARS AND THE STONES

Runes are a code, secret keys to the different facets of the whole interconnecting universe. Originated by the Germanic nomads who wandered the plains of northern Italy some 500 years before Christ, this compact and portable form of magic crossed the Alps and spread throughout northern Europe and Scandinavia. The twenty-four 'letters' of the *futharc* (an acronym of the first six letters of the runic alphabet) were used by the pragmatic Germans as a straightforward recording medium, as well as a shortcut to tapping the secrets of the universe. Each rune is a powerpacked symbol of one aspect of existence – for example, the fourth rune *As* means ash tree, but also signifies the tree of the world, the divine force that controls the cosmic order.

When the runes are cast, they combine, and the trained runemaster can read what has been, what is, and what influences are shaping future events. Authentic ancient runes, the portable arkana, were carved or painted on fresh-cut fruitwood and cast onto a white cloth for divination, but pebble or stone runes work just as well. Everyone should make their own runes – they have personal power, and they are free.

Runic astrology divides the sky into twenty-four segments, or seles, which correspond with the futharc. The seles modify the expression of planetary energy as each planet passes through them. The planets carry the attributes of the northern gods, and these too have runic associations.

As the sun signs do not coincide with the runic seles, they often come under the influence of two or more runes. The Libra runes are *Ken*, *Gyfu* and *Wyn*. *Ken* is the flaming torch of illumination, in this case the bright light of an intellect in harmony with the world, the radiance of inner spirituality and pleasure in worldly joys; it also provides the clear light of reason needed to make impartial fair judgement. *Gyfu*, meaning literally gift or talent, is the most important rune for Libra; it symbolizes the relationship between giver and receiver, and by extension the talent to foster cooperation and harmonious partnership. *Wyn* means joy, specifically the joyful well-being felt when you live in harmony with yourself and the world, balancing work and play. The runic image of Libra – a bright, balanced, creative soul, delighting in harmonious fellowship and happy cooperation for the achievement of shared goals – is remarkably similar to the zodiacal profile.

A small clutch of runes is associated with Libra's ruler Venus, whose northern equivalent is the goddess Frigg, consort of Odin. They are *Feoh*, *Ken*, *Jera*, *Peorth* and *Beorc*. For Libra the most significant is *Jera*, the twelfth rune of the futharc. Its literal meaning is year or season; it symbolizes the fruitful outcome of action undertaken in harmony with the natural order of things.

L I B R A

ZODIAC TREASURE

he zodiac treasure hoard may overflow with gorgeous gems, but it is guarded by grumpy and confused dragons, who squabble among themselves and cannot agree on which stone best fits which sign. However, the beguiling idea of a jewelled girdle encircling the zodiac is an ancient one, and may even be based on the twelve gemstones, one for each of the tribes of Israel, set on the breastplate of the Jewish high-priests of biblical times. Medieval astrologers felt reasonably sure of their ground and listed the gems

as follows, in zodiacal order: bloodstone, sapphire, agate, emerald, onyx, carnelian, chrysolite, aquamarine, topaz, ruby, garnet and amethyst. Catherine de Medici, the original power-dresser, was rumoured to possess a glittering belt of zodiacal gems.

As there is no real consensus in the matter, a new approach is needed. Consideration of the colour and characteristics traditionally attributed to each sun sign may lead to a satisfying match of sign with stone.

Libra's colours are gentle, harmonious pastels of blue, pink or green, the colours of Venus. Notoriously slow at coming to a final decision, Librans very sensibly opt for a selection of beautiful stones, to give them a wide choice and allow them to match their jewellery with their clothes in perfect harmony. And it is a first class selection: green jade and blue sapphires, turquoise and lapis lazuli (via Venus) and, intriguingly, coral. Coral is not a gemstone, but it is born from the sea, like Libra's patron goddess, and it comes in a rosy rainbow of delicate pinks and warm reds that reflect Libra's warm personality.

Librans can also wear opals, probably the only members of the zodiac who can. The opal's glamorous iridescence is the translucence of water trapped in its fissures, giving it a cloudy, creamy sheen not unlike the clouds that envelop the planet Venus. And opals are reputed to be loyal to Venus, bringing retribution down on the heads of those who cheat, lie or deceive in love.

When buying jewellery for Libra, be as extravagant as you can: Librans adore romantic gestures and luxurious indulgent chic. Don't forget that Libran women love earrings, the balanced symmetry of jewels on each side of the face – and adjusting them provides an unarguable excuse to preen innocently in the mirror.

EARTH'S HIDDEN POWER

Beneath the earth, in the realm of Pluto, lie the solidified energies, metals and crystals that hum with compacted potency.

The Libran metal is copper, a gently glowing decorative metal. Warm to the touch and light to wear, copper makes delightful jewellery, just right for everyday chic; the rich pinkish glow appeals to Librans' taste for the beautiful pastel colours associated with their ruler Venus. Copper's name comes from the ancient Greek word for Cyprus, where the metal was once abundant; and Cyprus was the birthplace of Venus.

Brass and bronze, both alloys of copper, also attract Libra; after all, the old-fashioned scales and weights that symbolize the birth sign are usually made of brass. Look out for a pair of elegant brass candlesticks symmetrically placed on the mantelpiece; Librans love to entertain in the warm, romantic gleam of candlelight. The welcoming intimate glow that lights most Libran homes will be

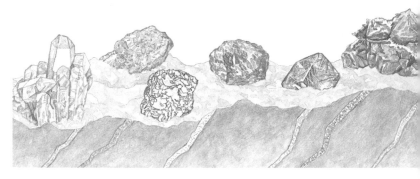

enriched by coppery-coloured planters or bronze-glazed terracotta pots filled with beautiful and unusual flowers or foliage deftly arranged by creative Libra.

Crystals are chemical elements compressed over millenia into dense, solid form, storehouses of electromagnetic energy. Lucky Librans, who prize beauty, benefit from a positive trove of crystals, all in the beautiful pastel colours beloved of Venus subjects: light green jasper, a joyful stone promoting the calm frame of mind that allows reasoned assessment of any situation; jade, which strengthens the kidneys, balances the emotions and encourages clarity of thought; pinky-red rhodochrosite and rose quartz – the 'love stone' – which stabilize the emotions and promote the proper balance of self-esteem and compassion.

Libra also has access to Venus's stones. Turquoise is the calming crystal, bringing harmony and balance to the whole body. After turquoise, blue lace agate, traditionally associated with the feminine principle, is the crystal for Venus. It tones and strengthens the whole body, helping Libra to build up the courage to finally make decisions.

LIBRA ON THE CARDS

ometimes called the Devil's Picture Book, the tarot was probably created in the twelfth century, but its origins are suitably shrouded in secrecy. There are seventy-eight cards: twenty-two in the Major Arcana, a gallery of enigmatic archetypal images from the Fool via the Wheel of Fortune to the World; and fifty-six in the Minor Arcana, divided into four suits – coins, cups, swords and batons (or wands).

Tarot cards, being one of the ways to explore the human psyche, have an affinity with the zodiac sun signs, and cards from the Major Arcana and the court cards from the Minor Arcana are associated with specific signs. If two cards are assigned, they should be considered together, but in some cases only one is appropriate.

Unsurprisingly, Libra is represented by Justice, the eighth card in the Major Arcana. Justice is shown as a mature, clear-browed woman, enthroned symmetrically between the twin pillars of integrity and impartiality, balancing the scales of justice in one hand and firmly holding the double-edged sword of retribution in the other. She is not blindfolded, as she represents all-seeing divine justice, the spirit behind our personal moral decisions, the choice between positive and negative, right and wrong, the spirit rather than the letter of the law. When overturned, Justice means bias, partiality, corruption and prejudice.

Libra's ruler Venus is associated with the Empress, the symbol of the creative female principle, the earth mother, queen of harmony and unification, guardian of feelings, emotions and intuition. A second influence comes from the Lovers, a complex card which symbolizes the dilemma for the self faced with the two seemingly opposing aspects of Venus: mother and wife. If life is to continue, individuals must strike out on their own; but the urge to stay comfortably at home, where love is certain and unconditional, is often overwhelming. Gentle Venus poses the dilemma, but is also the source of the answer, the spur of irresistible sexual desire fired by Eros, her own son.

INDEX